i

AWAKEN
THE
FIRST LADY
WITHIN

A Revolutionary New Approach to
Turning Your Passionate Purpose into Powerful Profits

FRANTONIA POLLINS

Founder of THE FIRST LADY LIFESTYLE ACADEMY for WOMEN ENTREPRENEURS

www.FrantoniaPollins.com

INTRODUCTION
TO THE
FIRST LADY
LIFESTYLE

Introduction to The First Lady Lifestyle

The First Lady Lifestyle is a movement designed to empower & inspire 1,000,000 Women Worldwide, to conquer their fears about Money & Wealth; discover their own uniquely Divine & powerful purpose on the planet and create successful businesses that empower them to leave a Multi-generational Legacy of Wealth.

This is accomplished by developing yourself spiritually, mentally, emotionally, physically and financially which has been proven to lead to a happier, more balanced and fulfilling life. Personal development is also one of the essential elements to creating and sustaining a successful and profitable business.

Quite simply, the First Lady Lifestyle is about empowering women to consciously & powerfully create a successful life and business rooted in maximum personal & professional development.

In order to attain the First Lady Lifestyle it is essential that you know who you really are, while this might sound silly to some, very few women have taken the journey toward realizing their TRUE power & self-worth. Although we have made major strides in many areas, unfortunately we still live in a social culture which presupposes that women are "less capable" and therefore less valuable than our male counterparts. Our society teaches us that in order to achieve success, climb the corporate ladder, accomplish your goals, start & run a successful and profitable business we must diminish ourselves and dismiss our Divine feminine gifts of creativity & intuition.

Rarely if ever are women encouraged to explore and fully express all that we are capable of achieving without also being required to sacrifice our femininity. In many ways, we are even told to reject our innate internal system of *"knowing";* because intuition, emotion and compassion are not seen as necessary tools for success, especially in the business world or corporate America.

I am here to shake up the myths that have taught you that in order to be successful as a woman we must abandon our true nature and do it the way that the guys do it. I believe that the Most High created us, men & women, separate and unique for a reason. There are talents skills and abilities that are innate to me as a woman that are of extreme value in creating a fulfilling life **and** in running a successful business.

Take intuition for example, it is my opinion that intuition is one of the most valuable God given success tools in the Universe. Listening to your intuition can save your life; that still small voice within, that gut feeling will tell you, "I know that's the normal route that you take to work each day but today, don't go down that street. Take a different route." And low and behold you avoid a car accident or Intuition says, "I don't know why, but for some reason cross the street." And a split second later an erratic driver may run into a group of people sitting at a nearby bus stop. You just never know…. In most success trainings we are taught that these things have no value or place; they are rarely even mentioned.

Because of this, very few women truly know how much power and influence they REALLY have in bringing about a massive, revolutionary shift that will not only improve their individual lives, families & businesses; but it is this hidden power that will make our world a much better place for many generations to come.

In order to truly realize the difference you make in the world you must begin to challenge the long held thoughts, ideas and paradigms that hold you back from achieving what you want from your life and your business. You must fully develop yourself in all key areas in order to reach your full potential.

The First Lady Lifestyle largely depends on mastering a few basic skills and regularly implementing them to create balance in 7 key areas of your life.

Those 7 key areas of Empowered Focus are:
1) Success Mindset
2) Spiritual / Self Awareness
3) Total Health & Fitness
4) Love & Relationships

5) Career & Entrepreneurship
6) Conscious Wealth Creation
7) Leadership, Legacy & Life Purpose

Over the next few chapters I'll share with you a 9 step blueprint that has been proven to bring about balance and holistic success, not only in your business and work environment but in every key area of your life so that you can truly begin to live the First Lady Lifestyle.

The Four Driving Forces of the First Lady Lifestyle

The First Lady Lifestyle is built on a foundation supported by four essential & driving forces which are:

✓ Power
✓ Purpose
✓ Passion
✓ Profit

YOUR 9 STEP
FIRST LADY
LIFESTYLE
SUCCESS
BLUEPRINT

Your 9 Step FIRST LADY LIFESTYLE BLUEPRINT for SUCCESS

The 9 steps of the First Lady Lifestyle are:
- ❖ **F** - FOCUS on the Finish
- ❖ **I** - INSPECT what you expect
- ❖ **R** - RELEASE Your Powerful Potential
- ❖ **S** - SYSTEMIZE Your Life & Your Business
- ❖ **T** - TAKE Your Message to the Masses
- ❖ **L** - LIVE Life on Your Own Terms
- ❖ **A** - ASSEMBLE Your Success Team
- ❖ **D** - DECIDE That Wealth is the Legacy You will Leave
- ❖ **Y** - YIELD Only to Your Dreams

FOCUS
ON THE FINISH...
BUT START
AT THE BEGINNING

F – FOCUS on the Finish…but Start at the Beginning

Clarify Your Vision & Bring Your Goals to Life

The first step is to Focus on the finish…but start at the beginning to clearly identify your vision for your life, THEN create a vision for your business. That's right – **FIRST** clarify the vision for what you want your life to look like, THEN build a business that supports your vision for your life.

Do you desire a life where you are in control of your schedule? Would you like to travel the world and visit exotic places? Do you want to have a life where you are able to stay at home and raise your children? What memories would you like to create? Just EXACTLY what do you want your life to look like? How much success are your prepared to receive? How big are your dreams for your life?

Visualizing yourself living the First Lady Lifestyle is an excellent way to bring your goals to the forefront especially when you're trying to determine what matters most to you. Achieving your targets and goals is best accomplished when you can imagine every detail of what it is you truly desire. In order to achieve big things in your life, you must be willing to think big and stretch far beyond your comfort zone - FIRST in your mind.

When you can picture what your desired life is like, you can better determine the goals you need to set and achieve to get there. *All it takes are small steps toward your desired future self, and you can achieve the life you deserve!*

When you're busily working toward bringing your goals to life, you also feel happier and more fulfilled in your journey.

Follow these steps to bring your goals to fruition by envisioning what you want in life:

- *Close your eyes and vividly visualize what you desire for your future.* Get that idea, goal or dream so deeply rooted in your imagination that you can literally close your eyes and see it. Where do you see yourself in six months, a year or five years? Try to think as far ahead as you comfortably can. Do you see yourself with a family, children, a successful business owner, a world traveler in five years?

   Try to have as vivid a visualization as you can. Pay attention to every detail, and let your dreams come to life in your mind, showing you what matters most to you. Think about where you want to be in the future and how you want to get there.

♣ *Create a Vision board* - Take it a step further so that when you open your eyes you can see it, what do I mean by that? – Most people wait until the end of the year because they think that that is the perfect time to start visualizing and planning for the things they want next year, but I say that every day is the perfect day or time to clarify and create your vision. Go out and make the investment in a white board, poster board and magazines, glue sticks & markers. You can even go to your local library and get old magazines that they are selling or giving away for free. Those magazines will have pictures and articles of things that you desire for your life and your business. CREATE a tangible, visual "map" of what your mind ultimately desires for your life. Once completed, place your vision board in a place where you will see it several times a day – EVERY day

♣ **Write the Vision, Make it plain!** Use as much detail as you can when jotting down what you remember. Write down the most important achievements that you focused on, but also the details about each. What matters most to you?

Write down everything you envision, something about writing it down in your own handwriting activates the subconscious mind. Use an ink pen with blue ink as something about the color blue activates the imagination. Listening to Classical Baroque music during this process will activate both the right (creative / feminine energy) and the left (analytical / masculine energy) brain.

Note the things that stood out in your visualization. Did you own your own home? Were you raising a family? Did you have a profitable business that made you happy? What other details stood out? How did you feel?

Once you have written it down, post it in a place where you will see it EVERY SINGLE DAY!

🐾 **Create a list of bullet points.** Do this for each separate achievement that you wrote about following your visualization. For example, if one of your achievements is "I own my own home," then you can list things like you are successfully saving for a down payment, that you're making monthly mortgage payments, and you have a business that generates a steady income.

🐾 **Break each of these bullet points down into goals.** For example, if one bullet point was to save for a down payment for the home you visualized, how can you get there? Create savings & income goals that will allow you to work toward having a down payment for your home.

🌑 Then break it down into no less than 3 daily action tasks – I use a dry erase marker and I write on my bathroom mirror the 3 tasks that I will complete that day toward the accomplishment of the goal that I have set.

🌑 **Lay out your plan.** Once you have a list of long term, medium term, and short term goals in mind, create a plan accordingly. How will you achieve these goals? How will you bring the life that you visualized into existence? *Divide your large goals into achievable steps.*

🌑 *Put a date on it!* I've seen so many people who NEVER reach their goals because they continually say I'm going to do, I'm going to do but they never get it done and 5, 10; 20 years have passed them by. Put a date on it and hold yourself to that date!!

🌑 *Get an accountability partner!* Once you have put a date on it, tell somebody so that they can hold you accountable. Give them permission to hold you accountable for achieving the goals & the dreams that you've set for yourself. I use my mastermind group for this.

♟ **Put your money where your mouth is.** Make a monetary investment in partnering with someone who is going to help you to make it happen. Be it a coach, a book, a training system, Personal development CD series – make the investment in gaining the tools that you need to be a success. Put your money where your purpose and your mission is.

♟ **Start achieving goals today.** Put your future plans into action today. Vow to take a small step each day toward the future you have envisioned. ***Move forward every day,*** even if you are only taking small steps at a time.

♟ **Commit!** Commit to doing absolutely everything that it takes before you even know what it takes. That means focus on the "what" and the" why" and don't worry about the "how." I know that this may seem a bit strange to you at first but right now, the how is none of your business. Focus on the "what" by asking yourself, "What is the step that I need to take TODAY?" Once you are clear about what that step is, take corresponding action. Tomorrow when you wake up, the only question you need to ask yourself is, "What is the step that I need to take TODAY?"

♟ **Trust** that everything that you need will either be revealed or attracted into your experience to help in the creation of your success.

♣ **Revisit your plan consistently.** Visualizations, dreams, and hopes change over time. Revisit the plan that you laid out and the future goals that you dreamed up on a consistent basis to ensure their relevancy over time. It's okay to change your dreams and goals based on your needs and desires as they change.

♣ **Celebrate** EVERY Victory!!

Self-Reflection

Action Steps

1)

2)

3)

4)

INSPECT
WHAT YOU
EXPECT

I – INSPECT What You Expect

Your Mind is Your Biggest Asset

The first step to discovering your potential is to realize that no matter your physical, financial or environmental limitations you, I and the vast majority of humanity has one very important asset in common: Our Mind.

Our mind can work with us and for us to help us reach our goals. Once we unlock the keys our mind holds, we have the opportunity to do the following:

- ***Learn to override the fears of failure***
  and not being good enough. To let go of social phobias and the hold of limiting beliefs.

- ***Discover the talents and gifts***
  We were given and how we can develop them.

- ***Learn how to spot new opportunities***
  To develop personal growth and learn new skills.

- ***Set & achieve POWERFUL goals***
  You had always thought were the goals of dreamers, and then meet those goals.

♚ *Develop a strong sense of purpose* and direction. Learn the value of your life in this world and what a difference your new life can make.

Become someone who loves to face a challenge and then meet it, and overcome it. You'll discover the fun in conquering the mountains of challenge in your own life and not taking the status quo as an acceptable standard anymore.

Why is having a SUCCESS MINDSET So Important?

Your ability to get to where you want to be and to live a life of purpose is in direct proportion to your ability to exercise mind control. It helps you to place your goals inside your subconscious, and then the process becomes a lot easier. The ideas and activities in this book will help to expand your mind to better embrace the probability for achieving the success you desire.

The ability to harness the power of your mind and control your thought processes is one that all successful people throughout the ages have used. It's the common denominator of all successful people whether they are business owners or world class athletes. Research in the ability to drive past our own limiting beliefs has shown that if we get the mind on track, the rest will follow.

You hear it all the time: "success is a state of mind." There are people who would argue that success is a natural result of proper planning, preparation and focused action, and that viewpoint certainly holds a grain of truth - but there are also many exceptions to disprove that "rule." Have you ever wondered how two people can attempt the same objective in the same way and only one of them succeed? Is it sheer luck? Is if timing? How about tenacity? More often than not, it's a person's mind-set that determines whether they fail or succeed.

What is a mind-set, anyway? Typically a mind-set refers to your **predominant** state of mind day to day. It's what you think about, focus on, and expect from your daily experiences. Think negatively, expect the worst, feel pessimistic about your options and that's exactly what you'll seem to draw into your life. Likewise, when you think positively, expect the best and focus on a successful outcome and you get it most of the time.

Makes sense, right? But how exactly does this work? Why is a success mind-set so important? There are three big reasons:

1) *A success mind-set boosts your confidence and self-belief.*

A lack of belief in oneself usually comes along with a sense of powerlessness and futility, which is the exact opposite of a success mind-set. Lack of confidence means you see no point in trying to be successful because it won't happen anyway, right? Obviously, this type of mind-set is a recipe for failure in any endeavor.

Having a true success mind-set, on the other hand, means you believe in yourself and your capabilities. You believe you can succeed at nearly anything you try, and you're willing to give it your best shot. Even better, the more you do try, the more confidence and self-belief you build - until you're virtually unstoppable!

2) A success mind-set strengthens your determination.

Without a success mind-set, one failure is enough to convince you that pursuing your goals is a waste of time. Tenacity and determination don't exist in your world. If you don't become a raging success the first time you try, you surmise that it simply wasn't meant to be. Unfortunately, few things worth having are obtained so easily!

A success mind-set, however, strengthens your awareness that a failure is not the end of the story - it's just one more way that didn't work out the way you planned. In fact, a true success mind-set makes it obvious that the only true failure occurs when you stop trying.

3) A success mind-set encourages fruitful actions.

Have you ever found yourself wandering in circles because you didn't know the best way to approach a specific goal? Perhaps you had an idea of the best course of action but you felt intimidated by some of the action steps required. As a result, you may have kept sabotaging your efforts as you searched in vain for an easier or less frightening way to your goal.

With a true success mind-set, you'll always know the most effective action steps that will lead directly to the accomplishment of your goal. As already discussed, you'll also have the inner confidence and determination to pursue them - which is a sure recipe for . . . you guessed it; success!

If I had to sum up how to develop a success mind-set into as few words as possible, I'd say this:

- ♟ Go for your dreams.
- ♟ Think positively.
- ♟ Believe in yourself.
- ♟ Believe you can do better.
- ♟ Learn, grow and develop yourself.
- ♟ Be willing to take chances.
- ♟ Give it your all.
- ♟ Expect the best in every situation.
- ♟ Be willing to fail.

♟ When you fall down, get back up and try again.

Keep doing that and you can't help but become successful, from the inside out.

Take corresponding action

A life without purpose is a life without richness, depth and reason. However you need to direct the purpose to ensure your dreams are realized. There is little point in investing the time and effort into discovering what you want to be, see or experience if you then do nothing with it.

Whatever you have now, in whatever amount you hold in your hands will only increase the more you use it. We have a chance to write our own life stories into something that others will want to follow and look to. But it doesn't happen just by dreaming- you need to act as well. If you want to have a positive impact on others, you'll do so by demonstrating your purpose & living a passionate life.

The key is to be as specific as you can about what your actual purpose is. For example many entrepreneurs think their purpose or passion is to become rich, when in fact it is to initiate, develop and create new ideas. Or maybe it is to be of greater service to the world in a way that only you can. The wealth is just one of the measurements or byproducts of that success.

Find what it is that expressly drives you, deeply moves you and therein you will discover your chief purpose. For instance, though you may want a lot of money- ask yourself why is that? What will having the money enable you to do? Is your chief goal to provide greater opportunities for your family? Or is it to have the freedom to spend your life serving a cause you believe in?

Self-Reflection

Action Steps

1)

2)

3)

4)

RELEASE YOUR POWERFUL POTENTIAL

R –RELEASE Your Powerful Potential

Discover Your Full Potential

Each one of us has potential lying innate inside of us. The brilliant part is each one of us has a potential that is uniquely our own. It's a mad mix of our mindset & philosophies, our environment, genetics or the way our body has been designed and the talents we were born with. Each one of us has something different, some gift to impart to this world

No matter what innate talents you were born with, no matter the family you were born into or the money you have made or lost, not matter the times of difficulty or lucky breaks, nothing will get you to where you want to be better than understanding and ACTIVATING your full potential.

I'm sure we've all heard the age old "woman who gets lucky story", or the "how I changed the world with my bare hands tale." These breakthroughs come from one important factor- the women who succeed are the women who learn how to tap into and fully embrace something innate inside them, so that they can live and breathe their dreams. ACTIVATED potential is the breaking factor in every story of success.

Of course, the first step is discovering just what your potential is. For some this is an instinctive process, often helped by a watchful parent or teacher that spotted something in us from an early age and called it into being.

For others, it's a struggle to identify. That can be for a range of reasons. We often have an instinct inkling of what we want to do as young children. This can be torn from us or pushed down by parental disapproval or expectations that don't match our own natural talents. For instance you may have been created as a creative person who loves to put colors and designs together, but come from a long line of successful accountants and business owners. There may be an expectation that you'll be working in business as you become an adult.

Environment can also play a part. We often learn about what we are good at through trying new things. If you lived in an area where there weren't a lot of options, or you didn't have a lot of money to pay for classes or for travel, then you may have not experienced the things you are naturally good at

Sometimes our very ambition, mixed with false belief can get in the way. Michael was a talented and creative designer who loved to put concepts together. However he was raised in a poor family and had experienced that embarrassing feeling of frequently being the only kid in his class without cool shoes, or the latest gadget. While he loved design he felt it couldn't make him money so he went for more traditional methods such as finance and accounting. No matter how hard he stuck at it he found himself stressed, unhappy and even worse, and poor as he couldn't seem to climb up the ladder to success.

Finally in desperation Michael started to do some designing for friends on the side just to keep himself sane. At first it was a free thing, but as his designs were shown to others, people started to ask to pay him. He discovered that you could actually be doing something you loved AND get paid for it. He just wishes he's known that a lot earlier.

Our potential can also be cut short by circumstance. If you are struggling to meet bills every week, and you have a family to support or other responsibilities, it can be difficult to see your way out of it to unlock that missing key and find success in the things you were born to do.

Whatever the reason or reasons that have brought you to want to unlock your potential, the most important thing from here on in is that none of that has to matter. For every time you've struggled and stressed that you'll never find your passion and then be able to use it, there is a person who has learnt to. And if they can do it, well you can too.

The Journey to Passion

"When work, commitment, and pleasure all become one and you reach that deep well where passion lives, nothing is impossible."

Like the majority of the world, you probably followed the path of "normal" – you went to school, got a 9 to 5 job drawing a good paycheck, you met the man of your dream, got married, have a good family and all's well with the world. But deep inside, you feel like you are going nowhere fast. You are actually stagnating in your career, the job isn't moving upward and you've hit the proverbial glass ceiling. And mentally and spiritually something is missing.

Passion! The one quality that textbooks, instruction manuals and company procedures will never talk about. Everyone is in such a hurry to make you fit perfectly into the "machine like" a well-oiled gear that they forgot you are a Spiritual being having a living, feeling, human experience. At times, even you have forgotten.

Ask yourself. If you had 10 million bucks in the bank, how would I be of service to the world? What kind of work would I be doing? Would I chuck this humdrum job and move on to something really exciting; something that I have always wanted to do?

Then ask yourself – why am I not doing that right now? Is it because of peer pressure or because I don't want to move out of my comfort zone? Don't want to rock my boat? You are half asleep in your boat already and in a few years; you could be put out to pasture! If the boat rocks now, you could be jerked awake and come to your passionate senses.

In the aftermath of the recession of 2008, myself along with millions of women lost their jobs. Many of us took up new vocations or started businesses of our own and suddenly found that we were finally following our dreams. Many of us are now highly successful and we are passionately living life on our own terms ourr new found professions.

. Identifying your Passionate purpose is an amazing journey and prosperity is just one of the landmarks on this route! If you are feeling unfulfilled, you don't have to wait for dire straits to rock you out of your present state. You can decide right now, that you want to live and work passionately and pursue your worthwhile purpose Get ready because this will be the ride of your life!

So what is the real Deal about Passion?

For some a life lived passionately is second nature. They seem to know the direction they should go in almost from birth, and everything always seems to fall into place for them. They are like a cat falling from a roof- no matter what they always seem to land on their feet.

However for many people, it takes a sharp change, a crystal clear moment or a long journey of learning to find that same direction. Fret not, it can be learned, and you can discover it by spending some time investigating your own history.

If you want to succeed in life and business, you first must find your passion, then harness and use it to focus your dreams and vision.

The more you follow the path your passion leads you down, the more you achieve the goals you desire, and many different area of your life will begin to fall into place.

You MUST be willing to change

A person without passion cannot change for they have no motivation to change. While not everything we do is directly related to our passion (It's pretty hard to explain the link between doing the dishes and micro banking for example) However, if we are assured in our passion, we do all those extra tasks a bit more gladly, knowing that passion will drive us especially when we are feeling a bit stressed or we find tasks to be difficult and less enjoyable.

While you'll still need to *do* something every now and again that may not be enjoyable, the hope is that the passion for the thing you love will grow and help to carry you through. That is one of the secrets of living a life where you meet your full potential.

One of the best parts of living a life of where you develop your own potential is it becomes infectious. People want to be around someone with direction and purpose. By finding your passionate purpose you will have an affect on everyone else in your life- without you even planning on it.

How Do You Find Your Purpose?

As we are all different, we will all need different paths to help us find our passionate purpose. If you've struggled to find the direction you need to complete your destiny, if you've always felt you were made for something, but a little unsure what it was then try some of the following ideas to explore what your purpose may be.

Everyone has a purpose, and there is potential in each of us. It's just a matter of exploring and investigating a little to discover it.

Know what you have in life

The first step you should take is to determine what you already have in your life, for example what are your best qualities, what are your particular talents and how could you develop further? Sit down and write an honest assessment of yourself in order to be able to expand on personal improvement. If you think that you might not be honest with yourself then ask family members or friends to give you some insight, but above all be totally honest with yourself in all areas, improvements can only be made if you can find ways in which to improve or branch out. Determine what it is you want to expand upon or develop in your life, the areas which could be better, where you could improve and what skills if any you need to learn in order to be able to accomplish your goals.

Go out on a limb

If you want to be successful in life, it is important that you push yourself every step of the way throughout life, never just sit back and rest on your laurels and be content with what you have achieved so far in life. You should continually be looking for ways in which you can improve your life and yourself to achieve and get more from life, develop yourself to your full potential and beyond. Think of yourself as a tree, the tree starts out as a sapling growing upward and expanding outward, continually branching out in all directions, and laying strong foundation roots deep underground, trees never stop growing and neither should you. Continually pushing yourself throughout life and going out on a limb is the key to being a total success in whatever you choose to do with your life.

What terrifies you?

It's an interesting concept but what you don't like, or what you fear may be the very thing pointing to your destiny. It's like the concept of yin and yang-there are two sides to each coin. The fear may originate from blocking off an early passion that you were unaware of.

🦋 Write a list of your fears and the negative feelings that come from them. Then look at that list and see if there is an opposite charge to the fear. For example, if you are terrified of public speaking, but love to share your ideas, then you may be well suited to expressing yourself through the written word.

🦋

When are you most afraid of failing?

Those things that are important to us hold a great deal of weight to how we see ourselves and our success. If you are scared at failing at something, you'll often avoid it at all costs. But those things we are scared to fail at are often the very things we most want to do.

Explore the times you've said no to something, or avoided something because you've been scared of showing yourself to not be good at it.

Who energizes you?

If you've only got people around you who tear or wear you down and you struggle with feeling good about yourself when you are around them, then you need to change that dynamic.

Make a list of the people who inspire you? What sort of people make you want to grab life and live it completely? Who is it that adds a little light into everything.

The people we are attracted to, who we want to spend time with, reflect not only where we are now, but where we want to be. Align yourself with people living a full life and their enthusiasm will rub off and help to ignite your own passion. Seek out people you respect, and work beside them- serving them. That is the very best way to learn. If you can't find anyone like that around you, devour books about people you admire and learn by proxy.

When will you get there?

It can be incredibly frustrating when you can see where you want to end up however each journey starts with one small step in front of the other. The end destination isn't the only thing you need- you must break it right down into manageable chunks. You may start with a small passion in something really simple that you don't think much of, and then it explodes and evolves into something else entirely. Enjoy that process, and trust it. The lessons we learn along the way as we explore our purpose are never wasted.

If you are naturally visionary, having to wait it out sometimes can be incredibly frustrating. However learning to temper your impatience and lay it aside helps you get there faster. Remembering that there is a season for everything you do help.

Self-Reflection

Action Steps

1)

2)

3)

4)

SYSTEMIZE
YOUR LIFE
& YOUR
BUSINESS

S –SYSTEMIZE Your Life & Your Business

Life Balance Requires Discipline

We can all benefit from having discipline in our lives, discipline helps us tell wrong from right as children when growing up and when we reach adulthood we still benefit from being self-disciplined. Self-discipline helps us to lead a happier, healthier lifestyle when used in many aspects of life, it is when we allow ourselves to do just as we please, that things start going wrong and our health suffers.

Self-discipline isn't about denying yourself, it is about making wise choices for our own benefit, the food we eat every day and the amount of exercise we do is dependent on how disciplined we are we with ourselves. While we all understand that the choices we make comes down to how healthy we are, we don't always make the wisest choices, and while this is ok every now and again if we lose all self-discipline it soon starts to show on our health and probably our waistline too.

Very often we make pacts with ourselves to start leading a healthier lifestyle and start making changes, this usually occurs at the start of the New Year as a resolution. While some stick to their guns and do make changes and keep up with those changes, the majority of us fall short and go back to our old ways. Being self-disciplined isn't easy, it takes a lot of willpower, especially if you need to make many changes to your lifestyle, but it's not impossible.

Here are some tips to help you stay on course and develop more self-discipline in all aspects of your life.

- Understand that the choices you make in life are yours and yours alone, you can't blame others for your failure if you lack self-discipline
- If you make mistakes in life, learn by them, pick yourself up and practice being more self-disciplined with yourself in the future
- Set yourself goals that are realistically achievable, once you have written out your goals make sure that you do everything in your power to stick to them and achieve them. Goals go a long way to encouraging you to discipline yourself.
- Always finish any task you set about doing before moving on to start another
- Avoid temptation from others around you to deviate from what it is you want to achieve, they may lack self-discipline but don't be swayed to following their ways
- Taking up a new sport, particularly one that requires a lot of self-discipline to excel at is an excellent way of improving yourself
- Notice the benefits you have gained from practicing self-discipline, keeping a journal is an excellent way of achieving this

- Imagine the consequences that being un-disciplined brings
- Your willpower is at its lowest when you feel stressed so take it easy, learn how to relax
- Take notice of when and why you start to go off track and deviate, again a journal can help you to keep track of these times
- Use affirmations to help you in times when you are frustrated or doubt yourself

How to manage your schedule and stay stress free

In today's busy world staying on top of things and being able to successfully manage your schedule is essential if you want to remain stress free, a schedule is all about planning your day more efficiently which ultimately ensures that you get everything accomplished that you wish to. The most efficient way to do this is to list your time and tasks in order of priority and determine what top priority is and to set out goals in your life that you want to accomplish.

Determining goals and priorities

In order to be able to manage your time more efficiently and get the most out of your day you must be able to be in control of your life and decide exactly what it is that you want out of life and what you need to do in order to reach what you want. The next decision is managing your priorities efficiently; you do this by determining what is more important to you. The next step is analyzing what you do with your time by finding out exactly how much time you spend on a particular task in life, a journal will help you greatly with this part and you should make a list of your schedule and daily life and determine exactly how long you take on certain activities. Activities you should include could be working, studying, exercising, sleeping and relaxation, once you have done this you can then go on to evaluate the use of your time and determine the best schedule for making better use of it.

Matching available time with your priorities

In order to best manage your time and make your day more efficient you need to take a look at the detailed list you prepared and use your time to match your priorities. As well as taking into account the amount of time you actually spend on each task you should also ask yourself if you are spending enough quality time on a task. A good example of this would be that if you studying then are you studying when you are likely to take in more information or is studying fitted in whenever you can, if you are leaving studying until the end of the day then you are likely to be tired and wont concentrate as well as you would earlier on in the day.

Tips for managing your time more efficiently

- Break down large tasks into smaller ones and tackling each individual part one at a time can ease the stress considerably than facing one larger task
- Get rid of routine tasks, if a task is done just out of routine instead of necessity then eliminate it if possible.
- Look at your habits to see if they could be changed, maybe you could do certain things different ways and save yourself some time in the process.
- Evaluate yourself to determine if you are a morning person or night person and organize tasks to use whatever time suits you best.
- Learn to say the word "no" when asked to do something for someone, don't be continually put upon by others who know you cannot refuse them, its ok doing favors but it can take considerable time from your day.

Time Management: The Key to a Successful Home-Based Business

Home-based businesses have provided income for families long before the internet. However, the internet has made opening and operating a home-based business easier than ever. These new businesses can provide you the opportunity to earn a substantial income in the comfort of your own home.

However, the picture isn't always so sunny. A home-based business requires work just like any other business. It's important to make the best use of your time to enable your business to bring you the profits and joy you deserve.

Being at home gives the feeling of comfort, relaxation, and escape from work, so it's very easy to lose focus and, as a result, get much different results than the ones you want from your business venture.

Making the Most of a Home-Based Business

So what's the fix? Developing a timetable to help manage your life at home will help ensure everything gets done when it needs to be.

Follow these tips to enable your time management tool to work effectively for you:

Use work time wisely

Allocate a specific time slot each day for work and use the time just for that. Avoid being distracted by TV or anything else. Remind yourself that you've scheduled enough time for everything, so work time should be just that!

Schedule enough rest time

Lack of rest can *significantly* impact the results from your home-based business. You'll start to feel tired and cranky if you're not well-rested, which will undoubtedly affect the quality and quantity of work you produce.

Avoid the temptation to cut into your rest time to get more done; use rest time for actually resting so your work doesn't suffer.

Include scheduled breaks

Once your timetable includes scheduled breaks during work slots, you'll have something to look forward to. You'll also have less of an urge to take "unscheduled" breaks while working.

Poor Time Management Can Lead to Unnecessary Challenges

Of course, how you manage your time at home will significantly impact the success of your at-home business. But what poor time management can also affect is "the rest of your life." That's right, working at home in a haphazard manner can really take its toll on other things.

> 👤 Family time and other important activities could be negatively impacted if you work in an ad hoc manner and don't reserve enough time for such things.

♟ Fitness, health, and diet also need your direct attention when you're a work at home earner. Not paying enough attention to those things could result in your health being in jeopardy. And that's the last thing you want when your only source of income is your home-based business!

It's very easy to get so absorbed in your home-based business and overlook the importance of other aspects of your life. Once you lose focus, your relationships will start to suffer and you may start neglecting your health. If you're working 16 hours per day, then you're most likely not exercising or eating properly. Nor are you spending time with your loved ones. Try to steer clear of this scenario!

Once you create a structured approach to your business and life in general, you'll find that you'll accomplish more, get more financial fulfillment from your business, and be able to achieve balance in other aspects of your life as well!

Self-Reflection

Action Steps

1)

2)

3)

4)

www.FrantoniaPollins.com

TAKE YOUR MESSAGE
TO THE
MASSES

T –TAKE Your Message to the Masses

Self-Employment Success: Market Yourself Like an Expert

Running your own business provides many perks over a regular 9-to-5 job. However, with great reward comes along great responsibility. **One of your responsibilities as an independent professional is marketing yourself effectively** to provide for both your business and family.

Follow these tips to market yourself like an expert, even if you're fresh out of the 9-to-5 workforce:

- Go for it. If all you do is dream up marketing schemes, you'll miss the opportunities to implement them. Instead, create one solid marketing plan and stick to it. Tweak your tactics according to your results.
- A marketing plan generally includes several marketing techniques, so choose several of your best ideas and start implementing them today. The faster you get out there and start peddling your business, the sooner you'll begin to increase your revenue.
- Exude confidence.

- When you're confident, people tend to trust your professionalism more than someone who seems timid and unsure of himself.

🐾 ***Present yourself with poise, professionalism, and ease.*** Always maintain confidence in the offerings of your business and your ability to succeed as an independent professional.

🐾 Test different techniques. Spread your marketing efforts across a number of different strategies. If one or two tactics are less successful, the success of other marketing efforts will keep your business afloat while you determine what gives you the best results.

🐾 Network like a pro. Jump at the opportunity to attend networking events related to your industry. It's one of the best ways to find clients and make industry contacts that may hire you at a later date or recommend you to their colleagues.

🐾 ***Attend workshops and seminars.*** You may have to pay a fee to attend conventions or events, but they are often well worth the price. You're paying to chat with a roomful of your target clientele. ***Even one new customer may enable you to earn back the cost and then some.***

🐾 Always bring a large stack of business cards and prepare an elevator speech. Sometimes, you'll only get a few minutes to chat with potential big-budget clients. So leave a lasting impression by displaying professionalism and confidence.

🔖 Do a bit of legwork to find out the proper dress code. Obviously, it's best to be overdressed than underdressed, but you'll feel silly sitting in a room full of people in cardigans and khakis while you're in a black Armani business suit.

🔖 *Search online photo sharing sites like Flickr for pictures posted by people that have attended the event you are interested in.* This way, you'll see firsthand what the regular attendees deem to be appropriate attire.

Marketing your business is an ongoing task that should be addressed regularly throughout the year. The more you market your business, the more you increase your exposure, make a name for yourself in the local community, and meet your financial goals.

Marketing is to your business what food is to the human body; without it, it's impossible to survive. Begin implementing these tips today to find success in your marketing and increase your revenue to new heights.

Go Global with the internet
5 Legitimate Ways to Make Money Online

The internet offers numerous opportunities for you to make money online. Unfortunately, the internet can also be a minefield of scammers. Because of this, many who have dreamed of earning a part time or full time income from home have given up. If you're dreaming of a way to supplement or replace your income at home, you can do so if you know where to look.

Try one or more of these ways to make money online:

Freelance your expertise.

If your specialty lends itself to freelancing remotely, take advantage of your scheduling flexibility and begin seeking paid work online. If possible, ask your current employer or existing clients if they'd be comfortable allowing you to work from home.

Careers that often work well with freelancing include writing and editing, consulting, marketing, transcription, medical coding, web/graphic designing, voiceover work, and programming.

Find clients by optimizing your website for the search engines, contacting local businesses, applying for gigs on Craigslist, and applying for freelance job openings on bidding sites.

Some of the most popular bidding sites for freelancers are Odesk.com, Elance.com, Guru.com, Rentacoder.com and getafreelancer.com.

Affiliate marketing

Affiliate marketing is selling the products of others online for a commission. If you're inconsistent and sporadic with your efforts, you'll be lucky to make $100 in a year. But *if you're consistent and diligent with your efforts, the sky's the limit on your earnings.*

♟ Affiliate marketing is all about doing your research before you begin trying to make money and most of your money will come by planting seeds. In this industry, "seeds" are affiliate links. *The more affiliate links you have on the net, the more money you'll make.*

♟ It can take months to see serious income as an affiliate marketer. It's common to earn just $10 for the first few months of your affiliate marketing career, and then all of a sudden to start earning $2,000, $4,000, or more per month.

Virtual assistant

A virtual assistant is essentially an office or personal assistant that serves their clients from home rather than a traditional office setting. You'll likely answer emails, set appointments, and spend time making various types of spreadsheets.

- ♟ Essentially, being a virtual assistant is like being a freelancer. **You can have multiple clients at once.** Generally, the pay rate ranges from $10 per hour as an entry-level assistant, to about $40 per hour for highly experienced ones.

- ♟ Like most freelancers, you can also find virtual assistant jobs on freelance websites and Craigslist.

Blogging

As a blogger, you're totally your own boss. But **with this freedom also comes great responsibility.** You're in charge of creating daily blog posts, driving traffic to your blog, and sourcing advertisers for your blog. For greater success, you'll also want to build a list of targeted subscribers.

- ♟ The income for a blogger varies widely. You're paid by advertising revenue, rather than on a per project basis. Plus, you can make money from selling your products or the products of others for a commission through your blog and newsletter.

Your income is directly correlated with your skills, efforts, and likeability.

🌑 Keep your day job for at least a year. It takes a while to build up income in a blog. *Some blogs can take two years or more to build up revenue that's equivalent to your current salary.*

Selling your own product.

The classic method of making money online is selling your own product. Whether you make aprons, clothing, and kitschy décor or you're selling manufactured cell phone accessories, *there's a place for your business on the internet.*

🌑 To make money online by selling products, you must market your business diligently. Employ search engine optimization tactics, start a blog for your business, ensure that your website is easy to navigate, and embark on an advertising campaign to attract buyers.

While there are still many scams on the internet, a bit of legwork can help you find legitimate ways to make money from home. *Seek forums for like-*

minded people online that can guide you in the right direction and help you steer clear of scams.

Remember that no legitimate work at home opportunity asks you to pay in advance to work for them. Above all, use discretion and proceed with caution. Give the above opportunities a try for a legitimate way to put more cash in your pocket and more freedom into your schedule!

Self-Reflection

Action Steps

1)

2)

3)

4)

LIVE
YOUR LIFE
ON YOUR
OWN TERMS

L – LIVE Life on Your Terms

Spiritual Wellness Can Create Balance in Your Life

Are you searching for deeper spiritual meaning in your life? You're not alone; the hectic demands of life in the 21st-century has made many people feel disconnected.

Perhaps what you need is a spiritual connection to bring about a sense of balance and completion in your life.

Many people confuse spirituality with religion and believe that spiritual wellness can only come from religious beliefs. However, spiritual balance comes from more than subscribing to a religion. Some people do seek religion for their spirituality, but spirituality can also be achieved without belonging to a specific religion.

How to Develop Spiritual Wellness

Essentially, developing spiritual wellness means working toward identifying what you believe in and how well those beliefs can give you inner strength through even the roughest patches in life.

When you've developed spiritual wellness, you can:

- Respond to others honestly, regardless of the situation.
- Express the values that you uphold and stand behind them at all times.
- Understand the meaning of life and become in tune with the meaning of your existence.
- Lead a fulfilling life.

How do we achieve spiritual wellness? Each of us has to develop our spirituality in own way. *Your chosen path may take you on a different journey than another's.*

When you're ready to begin your journey toward spiritual wellness, consider the following suggestions:

Question the purpose of your existence.

Ask yourself a few key questions as you go on a quest to achieve balance through spiritual wellness. *Self-exploration is the key to developing your spiritual balance.* Ask yourself:

- What defines me?
- What is the purpose of my existence on the planet?
- What things, people, and ideologies should I be committed to?
- What do I want out of life?

Connect to what's meaningful.

After you've answered those questions, your next mission is to connect to and identify with the things in life that you want to represent you. Do you believe in helping others? Is it your interest to sacrifice the physical aspects of life to gain spiritual strength? *Put the answers to the questions to work.*

- Contribute to a charity if you're inclined to help others.
- Go on a fasting mission to gain endurance and clarity of mind.

Test your limits.

When you take on challenges, you expand your understanding of a whole new myriad of possibilities for you. Testing your limits could involve many things. Here are some examples:

- Take on a physical challenge that ordinarily you wouldn't take on due to fear of failure, disappointment, or the challenge itself.
- Make a decision based on your beliefs even though you know it may not be popular.
- Have the strength to stand by those convictions even if others reject them.

Becoming spiritually strong involves believing in something. It involves identifying your purpose and working towards achieving that purpose. Most importantly, it involves becoming truly happy with your life.

Ultimately, the balance you seek will come when you satisfy your spiritual needs. By taking the steps outlined here, you can put yourself on the right path to spiritual fulfillment.

Achieving spiritual wellness isn't an overnight process. With persistence and dedication, you'll find yourself connecting with another aspect of your existence that you never realized. More and more things will become clearer to you and you'll start to experience true inner peace, no matter what challenges you're faced with!

Self-Reflection

Action Steps

1)

2)

3)

4)

ASSEMBLE
YOUR
SUCCESS
TEAM

A –ASSEMBLE Your Success Team

Success Coach, Mentors & Masterminds
All About A Life Coach

A life coach, or life skills coach, as they're occasionally called, is basically a personal trainer for your life. As the name connotes, these personal coaches work with persons to better assorted areas of their lives. Depending on your circumstances and how you decide to work with your coach, they can take on a number of roles. These may include motivation coach, personal development coach, executive coach, small business or career coach, or relationship coach. Read further for some details on what to look for in a life coach.

Basically, your coach is there to inspire and motivate you to do better, in a particular way. Commonly, you choose the areas that you want to work on (objectives) and your coach works with you to arrange change.

Pricing for professional coaches will differ from one coach to another. Individual coaches ascertain their own pricing, there are no laws covering life coaches so the costs that are charged are based upon what the market might bear. More experienced and accomplished coaches are more probable to charge a much greater fee.

It's one thing to find a life coach who's taken a training program and gotten certified as a life coach. But it's quite another for that person to becoming a good life coach. A good life coach will have the ability to assess an individual's or group's needs and help and advance them. They can work with their clients at any time in their growth and development process.

The measurement of the Quality of your Life is an increasingly crucial issue for your well-being. This should be an area your life coach will be helping you with.

Identifying your development needs can be thought-provoking. Often, we find ourselves viewing what training courses are available and deciding which of those would be most helpful. As a matter of fact, it's better to try and identify what the development need is and then to work out ways of meeting that need, which might or might not be a training course. Your life coach should be able to help you through this process and put you on the correct path for fixing what needs to be fixed.

A life coach can help you to deal with difficulties in making changes.

Why you must have a life coach

If you would like to achieve more or enhance your life then you should consider getting advice from a life coach. A life coach can be many things including your personal consultant, someone who listens or your manager, they can help to set you in the right direction in life, help you to get the most out of life and determine your goals in life and help you reach them.

The many ways you can benefit by having a life coach

- Help you to gain more control over your life
- Develop better strategies for managing your time.
- Reduce stress and increase your productivity by simplifying your life.
- Helping you to realize and maximize your Potential.
- Help improve your relationships with others
- Help you to prioritize tasks and meet deadlines more easily
- Help with important decisions you have to make in life
- Show you techniques to enable you to deal better in stressful situations
- Help you to balance your work and social life
- Help you to develop plans of action and life goals

A life coach can help in both professional and personal life and are there to help you obtain better results and gain a better quality of life in all aspects. Life coaches have been trained to adapt to listening, observing and then developing individual strategies to help people get out of the rut they find themselves in.

How to know when it's time to hire a life coach?

In order to determine if you benefit from having a life coach the first question you should ask yourself is "what do I wish to accomplish with a life coach?" if you can answer this question then a life coach would be able to work successfully alongside you to help you develop a strategy to obtain your goals. Life coaching is all about developing a partnership between the two of you and it is essential that you are able to be open to advice and constructive criticism; if you are not, then a life coach may not be the best option for you. Listed below are some questions that could help you determine if you could benefit from a life coach, if you can answer yes to any of them then you could possibly benefit from having a life coach.

- Do you feel there is a lack of support in your life?
- Do you have problems with low self-esteem issues?
- Do you feel everyone has a plan or goal in life but you?
- Do you feel you are going through a tough time and need a helping hand?
- Do you feel bogged down with deadline and don't know which way to turn?
- Do daily tasks make you feel overwhelmed?

♣ Do you feel as though the entire world is against you?

♣ Do you feel everyone knows the secret to being successful but you?

♣ Do you feel you could get more out of life or better yourself?

Self-Reflection

Action Steps

1)

2)

3)

4)

DECIDE
THAT WEALTH IS THE LEGACY YOU WILL LEAVE

D – DECIDE that Wealth is the Legacy that You Will Leave

Wealth Isn't for the Wealthy - Wealth is for the Smart!

Do you believe that being predisposed with the ability to become wealthy is the *only* way to earn good money?

Fortunately, the reality is that wealth belongs to those who are smart in the ways they go about claiming and creating it.

Being able to make money even without having that background from the onset is definitely attainable, as long as you put some thought and creativity into your wealth making opportunities. Making solid financial decisions and choosing sound investment options are simply the best ways to become wealthy once and for all.

Develop a Wealth Consciousness - Think your way to becoming rich

How we think goes a long way to how successful we are in life and we have the power to change our lives in every aspect including our finances. Simply by changing the way we think can change our outlook on our financial situation and while this alone will not make you a millionaire, it can greatly improve your situation and by believing that money can come to you will give it the opportunity to do so.

Have you ever stopped to think why those who are rich keep on getting richer; one of the reasons is that they think differently about money to those who have not got money. Negative thinking brings nothing but negativity and negativity will not bring money. However, thinking positively can change many situations in life and one thing the rich do is to always think positively. Here are some examples of the outlook and way of thinking that those with money have and what those without money think about the same situation.

The average person – If it sounds too good to be true then it probably is

The rich person – It sounds interesting, please tell me a little more

While we should all be wary of scams, the rich person is more willing to seek out an opportunity to draw more money in than the person with little money, sometimes the saying "you have to spend money to make money" is true.

The average person – 95% of all new businesses fail within the first five years

The rich person – I better look into all aspects of the business and make sure I do my homework, if I want to run a successful business

Starting out with negativity in mind is not the best way to get your business up and running, providing you have looked into your new business project and got advice there is no reason to think negatively about the prospects and success.

The average person – the grass is always greener on the other side of the fence

The rich person – there is a whole world of opportunities out there just waiting for me to discover them

The average person always allows themselves to think that they cannot do better and achieve what it is they want out of life, that only others can do that, by thinking negatively they are not giving themselves the opportunity to expand and are full of "what ifs" and "if only"

The average person - you have to have money in order to be able to make money

The rich person – you have to have a great idea in order to make money

While common sense dictates in some circumstances that to get your idea off the ground it can cost you money, a positive attitude towards the outlay of your money and the rewards it will bring you is the big difference between failure and success.

The average person – I tried that before and only failed, so it will again

The rich person – what do I have to do differently and change this time in order to for it to be a success

Again negativity comes into play; just because it didn't turn out as planned the last time doesn't mean that you should give up and not try again after sitting back and looking at the mistakes you made and altering for a different outcome.

All these thoughts have one thing in common a negative and a positive outlook on life and what you do with it, by simply changing your outlook you open up for yourself a whole new world and a whole lot more possibilities for you to change your financial situation.

Here are three simple, yet effective, tips you can apply to your life that can help to create the wealth you deserve:

1) Break down your big money goal.

"I want to be rich!" Just about everybody you can think of has said this at one point or another in his or her lives. Being wealthy is something that most of us dream about - however very few are able to achieve - because we look at it as a large, insurmountable goal. Remember:

🐾 *Looking at your desired achievement as an overwhelmingly huge goal makes it very difficult to obtain.* In fact, it almost always amounts to a mere dream if we overlook setting smaller, attainable goals towards that major goal. And that's one of the keys for becoming wealthy.

🐾 Break your financial goal into smaller, more achievable ones that you can set reasonable timeframes on. You'll be surprised to see how you progress towards your huge goal once you set smaller ones that are much easier to achieve.

2) Avoid using credit if you can't pay by cash.

One of the simplest and most effective tips for building wealth is to avoid credit. *And what that means essentially is avoiding credit if you see no way to repay it in the short term.* Remember:

🐾 If it isn't possible for you to have the cash to settle your credit card expenses each month, then *avoid making purchases with the card.*

♟ By choosing to purchase only what you can afford to purchase with *cash,* you can undoubtedly start to create wealth for yourself.

3) Live within your means.

Sure, there will be things you see that you want to do, acquire, or simply accomplish. However:

♟ If it's not financially easy for you to do something or acquire something, then perhaps you should leave it alone for the time being.

♟ It's very likely that something you aren't able to do this month or this year will be more than possible in the near future.

♟ ***You should only focus on doing things and acquiring things that you are financially able to without feeling stressed in the pockets.*** The more often you practice that approach, the closer you'll be to having financial freedom.

Creating wealth requires very little money and quite a bit of financial "smarts." The more reasoning, thought, and common sense you put into your financial decisions, the sooner you'll find yourself becoming wealthy. Count yourself amongst the masters of wealth by applying some creative thinking.

Achieve your financial goals by taking it in stride and believe that *you* are predisposed to the same wealth as anyone else!

Bringing in extra cash.

One stumbling block you may encounter is finding a way to earn the income you need to survive and thrive. However, with the right strategies and a determination to succeed, this stumbling block can be turned into a stepping-stone toward your success.

Many online and offline income strategies offer you the opportunity to realize your dreams if you'll take the first step today.

Use a hobby to become successful

Almost everyone has a hobby; a hobby is something which you take pleasure from doing and relieves boredom, stress and keeps you occupied in your spare time, however you can take some hobbies and develop them into successful businesses. Some people have started out with a hobby and built up a very successful business from the ground up by doing something that they, although some hobbies more than others naturally have more potential to thrive and expand. There are some points to consider when you are thinking of turning your hobby into a business.

Do you have the commitment?

While your hobby is something which you enjoy doing now in your spare time, would you have the commitment needed to stick with it if you were doing it full time, what's more do you have the time needed to commit to make a business work? Doing something when you feel like it for fun is a totally different thing than if you are relying on it for an income.

Financing

You will have to determine how much it is going to take to finance your hobby as a business and get it off the ground, how will you finance it is an important point to consider along with your knowledge of running a business in general. Do you have a head for business or are you going to need any help and how much help will you need and what is it going to cost?

Business management courses

If you have a head for business then you may need to take a business management course, while you may have what it takes and the know how to manage a business successfully you may need to get qualifications or learn skills in order to run your business successfully.

Attracting customers

If you are going to successfully turn your hobby into a thriving business then it is essential of course that people know about you and what you are offering, therefore you have to think about widening your customer base. The Internet provides an excellent opportunity to widen your customer base internationally; the Internet delivers what you have to offer to millions of people around the world by advertising your business on your own website. Some knowledge of coding is needed and you may have to hire someone to work with you to design and plan your site and not only that you then have to get it out on the web by way of promoting it on search engines and buying advertising space.

Preparing yourself for success

If all goes according to plan and you have thought your plan through your new business will bloom and blossom into a success, when this happens you will have to be prepared for the transformations that will take place. If your business expands then it may become too large for a one man operation and then you will be faced with a whole new set of problems to contend with such as finding bigger premises, hiring extra staff and meeting greater demand.

Self-Reflection

Action Steps

1)

2)

3)

4)

YIELD
ONLY
TO YOUR
DREAMS

Y - YIELD Only to Your Dreams

Leadership, Legacy & Life Purpose

When you are young, your motivation for working and living lies in larger income, better standards of living and in general having a good time. But as you grow older, your priorities change. You want something more fulfilling. You seek to achieve goals that you will be remembered for. A sense of urgency begins to set in as time passes. And the source of your passion arises from wanting to leave behind a legacy.

That legacy may take the form of social change brought about by your work. Or it can be in an enterprise or institution founded by you. Many successful businessmen set up foundations and trusts in the pursuit of noble causes. Thus they seek to perpetuate their name or family name for posterity. An invention or a new process or a novel product can also enshrine the maker's name in the books of history.

Temporal pleasures and petty rewards do not satisfy someone working at this level. His or her passion seeks loftier goals. The greater the goal, the more fervent the passion. Revolutionaries and freedom fighters like Mahatma Gandhi and Che Guevara struggled all their lives for the liberation of their countries. Their ambitions encompassed the lives of millions of their countrymen. The sheer magnitude of their legacy consumed their entire lifetime, but it was a passionate lifetime, with every day spent in pursuit of that goal.

How do you set about leaving behind your legacy? What is it that you feel strongly about? Write down your strongest emotions and issues. They may even lie outside your present work area. Start working on those issues. Educate yourself and acquire new skills if you have to, and get to work. It may be a simple project like improving your community, or a major reform of state laws.

Remember that all the great men and women who have brought about change did so with a heartfelt dedication to be part of something much bigger than themselves.

Self-Reflection

Action Steps

1)

2)

3)

4)

ABOUT THE AUTHOR

Frantonia Pollins is a leading authority on Women's Empowerment & Feminine Leadership. Affectionately known as "America's First Lady of Empowerment", Frantonia has studied, interpreted and in her own unique way, presented the Universal success principles of the most dynamic people to ever live.

With a zealous commitment to "re-introducing" women to their TRUE power, Frantonia Pollins is a compelling, compassionate & RESULTS oriented speaker, author & coach; who for more than 20 years has helped thousands of individuals to achieve their dreams.

On a personal crusade to inspire 1,000,000 Women (worldwide) to conquer their fears about Money & Wealth, discover their own uniquely Divine & powerful purpose on the planet and create successful businesses that empower them to leave a Multi-generational Legacy of Wealth, Frantonia's innovative work expresses her passion for helping women to tap into and use the infinite power that we all possess, a power that she believes can change the world.

Her latest initiative is the FIRST LADY LIFESTYLE ACADEMY, a year- long coaching intensive designed to guide women toward being powerfully positioned as "First Lady" in these 7 key areas of their lives.

1-Success Mindset
2-Total Health & Wellness
3-Love & Relationships
4-Spiritual / Self Awareness
5-Conscious Wealth Creation
6-Career & Entrepreneurship
7-Leadership, Legacy & Life Purpose

Frantonia has authored "One Powerful Question" a 3-book series that challenges the limiting beliefs that hinder our ability to fully live out our greatest potential. Her latest book entitled, "AWAKEN THE FIRST LADY WITHIN" is a must-have guide for every women who has ever dreamed of having a successful business that allows her to powerfully profit from her passionate purpose while creating a fully balanced lifestyle

www.ingramcontent.com/pod-product-compliance
Lightning Source LLC
LaVergne TN
LVHW021508080426
835509LV00018B/2441